CHURCH MUSIC SOCIETY PUBLICATION: 023A
Hon. General Editor: Richard Lyne

T0033742

for the Choir and Congregation of St. Mary's Church, North Leigh, Oxon.

Saint Mary's Mass

Music by ANTHONY CÆSAR

Kyrie

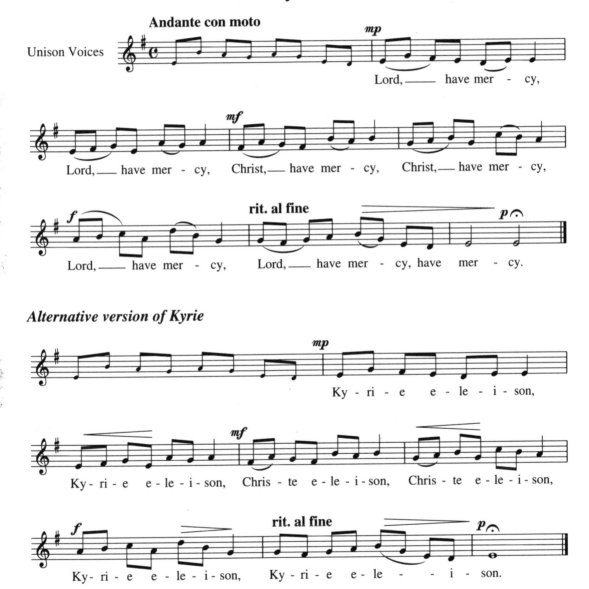

Alternative version of Kyrie

Gloria

For you— a-lone are the Ho - ly One, you a-lone are the Lord,—

cresc. you a-lone are the Most High, Je - sus Christ, with the Ho - ly Spi - rit,

allargando *ff* in the glo - ry of God— the Fa - ther. A - men. A - men.

Gospel Responses

mf Glo - ry to Christ— our Sa - viour.

mf *f* Praise— to Christ— our Lord.—

Sanctus – Benedictus

Andante solenne *pp* Ho - ly, Ho - ly, Ho - ly Lord, God— of pow'r and

più mosso *mf* *f* might, heav'n— and earth are full— of your glo - ry. Ho-san-na in the

mf high-est. Bless - ed is he who comes— in the name— of the

f *ff* Lord. Ho-san - na in the high-est, Ho - san - na in the high - est.

Acclamations

Agnus Dei

Acknowledgment

The *Gloria,* the *Sanctus,* the *Benedictus* and the *Agnus Dei* from *The Order for Holy Communion Rite A* from the Alternative Service Book 1980 are © International Consultation on English Texts and are reproduced with permission of the Central Board of Finance of the Church of England.

ISBN 0-19-395363-3

Origination by Jeanne Fisher, Ludlow, Shropshire
Printed by Halstan & Co. Ltd., Amersham, Bucks

Pack of 10 copies
Not available separately